RUNNING the WORLD

FOR THE AMAZING PEOPLE AT KATY'S PLACE -

THANK YOU FOR ALL THE BEAUTIFUL MEMORIES!

YOU ARE THE GIFT YOU CAME HERE TO GIVE.

SHINE YOUR LIGHT,

Melissa :)

MC²

RUNNING the WORLD

Marathon Memoirs from the Seven Continents

MELISSA CORLEY CARTER, PhD

BROWN BOOKS
PUBLISHING GROUP

Running the World
Marathon Memoirs from the Seven Continents

Brown Books Publishing Group
Dallas, TX / New York, NY
www.BrownBooks.com
(972) 381-0009

A New Era in Publishing®

Publisher's Cataloging-In-Publication Data

Names: Carter, Melissa Corley, author.
Title: Running the world : marathon memoirs from the seven continents / Melissa
  Corley Carter, PhD.
Description: Dallas, TX ; New York, NY : Brown Books Publishing Group, [2021]
Identifiers: ISBN 9781612545059
Subjects: LCSH: Carter, Melissa Corley. | Women long-distance runners--
  Biography. | Marathon running--Pictorial works. | Self-realization in women.
  | Quality of life--Psychological aspects. | LCGFT: Autobiographies.
Classification: LCC GV1061.15.C38 A3 2021 | DDC 796.4252092--dc23

ISBN 978-1-61254-505-9
LCCN 2020923389

Printed in China
10 9 8 7 6 5 4 3 2 1

For more information or to contact the author,
please go to www.ResilienceActually.com.

For my husband, Al, who made this book possible in so many ways.
India Lima Yankee, Papa Hotel.

Gentoo penguins on the Aitcho Islands in Antarctica.

Contents

Foreword

One in a Million and the Million-Dollar Tour

When I met Melissa, I was the technical director of a large Air Force optical research facility in New Mexico. It was late summer in 2004. She was on a mandatory interview cycle for her first assignment as a new lieutenant and Stanford University engineering graduate. I had received word that she had already stated her preference for assignment to a different directorate dealing with space technologies. I understood the reason why later on—her life's goal was to be an astronaut. I didn't have advanced notice of her visit; I had only received an email that morning with a short résumé and references. I was impressed. On paper, she had "the right stuff" to become a valued member of our team—passionate, dedicated, and productive.

We met at the laboratory support building, got into my car, and drove up the hill to the big telescopes. I've been in this business long enough (forty-nine years now) to immediately spot the good ones. Before we got out of the car at the end of the two-minute drive, I knew Melissa was in the GREAT category. She was interactive, very intelligent, got it the first time, and had that can-do, eager-to-get-started attitude. Of all the things I look for in potential job candidates, attitude is the most important. I thought to myself, "Is there any way I can convince her to change her preferred assignment?" We spent an hour looking at the big telescopes and complex optomechanical apparatus covering the large optical tables. The more we talked, the more I knew she was one in a million. We drove back down the hill, and as I parked the car, I said, "Well, that's the twenty-five-cent tour."

By some miracle of fate, Melissa ended up assigned to our group and exceeded my highest expectations for innovation, productivity, and performance as a team player. I gave her more and more responsibility and she devoured it. She led a big project that required both daytime engineering and nighttime operations. She had an old Chevy Suburban and often slept in it at the research facility, ready for action on a moment's notice. Her dedication went beyond the norm. On top of her mega work schedule, she had also started running, mentored by a super athlete on our team. It must have been hard to maintain balance in her life, but she did, and her book elaborates on this subject. Near the end of her assignment, and when I retired from government service in 2006, my colleagues were invited to write farewell notes on three-by-five-inch notecards. Melissa's note started with, "I will never forget the day I met you, when you drove me up the hill and gave me the million-dollar tour."

Running the World is more than a book about visiting all seven continents and running marathons. It's a book about achieving fulfillment in your life and preparing yourself for life's challenges. It's about building confidence in yourself. This book is about accepting the difficult hills in life and approaching them as "manageable chunks." It's about opening your senses and awareness. It's about discovering who you are.

Running the World is a page turner. Melissa's writing style reflects her inner being: intimate and personal, friendly and to the point. Easy reading, deep meaning. She develops a strong connection with the reader. She chronicles her five-year journey from the initial concept of running a marathon on every continent through the dedicated training, agony, victories, inner growth, beauty of nature, native residents and cultures, wildlife encounters, new friends, life-changing experiences, lunar and solar eclipses, to the last step across the finish line in Australia, completing marathons on all seven continents.

From Melissa's opening story, we learn that her kindness and concern for others outweighs her desire to win. Her philosophy—that life is about *how* you run the race rather than *winning* the race—continued during her marathons, especially at the Great Wall of China.

The China marathon was among the most grueling, with time deadlines to pass the twenty-one-mile mark and an eight-hour time limit to finish the race in what turned out to be sweltering heat. The course followed the steep grades of the hilly countryside, and the wall portion itself had more than five thousand stairs. Physical and logistical complications led Melissa to feel nervous about meeting both time requirements. However, the race's dire circumstances turned into a rewarding, character-building experience. On the day of the race, two opportunities presented themselves: the opportunity to be helped and the opportunity to offer help.

For me, this story is one of the most compelling in the entire book. For Melissa, this experience was one of the most significant in developing her life philosophy, and she does a great job of communicating that philosophy to the rest of us.

Melissa has a creative eye for photography. The book encompasses many stories about people, nature, wildlife, and the beauty this planet holds. The photography presented in these pages brings life and perspective to Melissa's stories and instills a feeling of place within the reader. It is clearly extra credit to Melissa to know that, in most races, she carried a small camera while running (mobile phone cameras were not really that good in this era) and paused long enough to take well-composed photos. Her real-time composition skills are quite remarkable.

Melissa describes a final hill challenge from her last marathon in Australia. You'll have to continue reading to understand how she took on this challenge and how she felt when she conquered it. Hills are an important part of the book. They present challenges that evoke solutions. They represent so many situations we encounter in life.

The title of the book, *Running the World,* has hidden meaning for me. Yes, the book is comprised of stories about the challenges of running marathons and the joys of visiting some of the most exciting places on this planet. However, it also imparts wisdom and philosophy to the reader, encouraging the visualization of one's personal challenges as hills to climb and goals to meet—guidance and philosophy for running *your* world.

Robert Q. Fugate, PhD
Albuquerque, New Mexico

"Flight to Venus"
© 2012 by Robert Q. Fugate. Taken June 5, 2012, from Continental Divide, New Mexico. Bob set out to photograph the transit of Venus (the black dot) across the sun. A serendipitous series of events led him to the one-in-a-million shot that captured an aircraft in flight as well. Ever the brilliant and curious scientist, Bob tracked down the flight information and sent a framed print of this photo to the captain of the United Parcel Service flight, who became known as Captain Planet. For the full story of this photo, visit https://www.rqfphoto.com/Events/Flight-to-Venus/. Photo printed with permission.

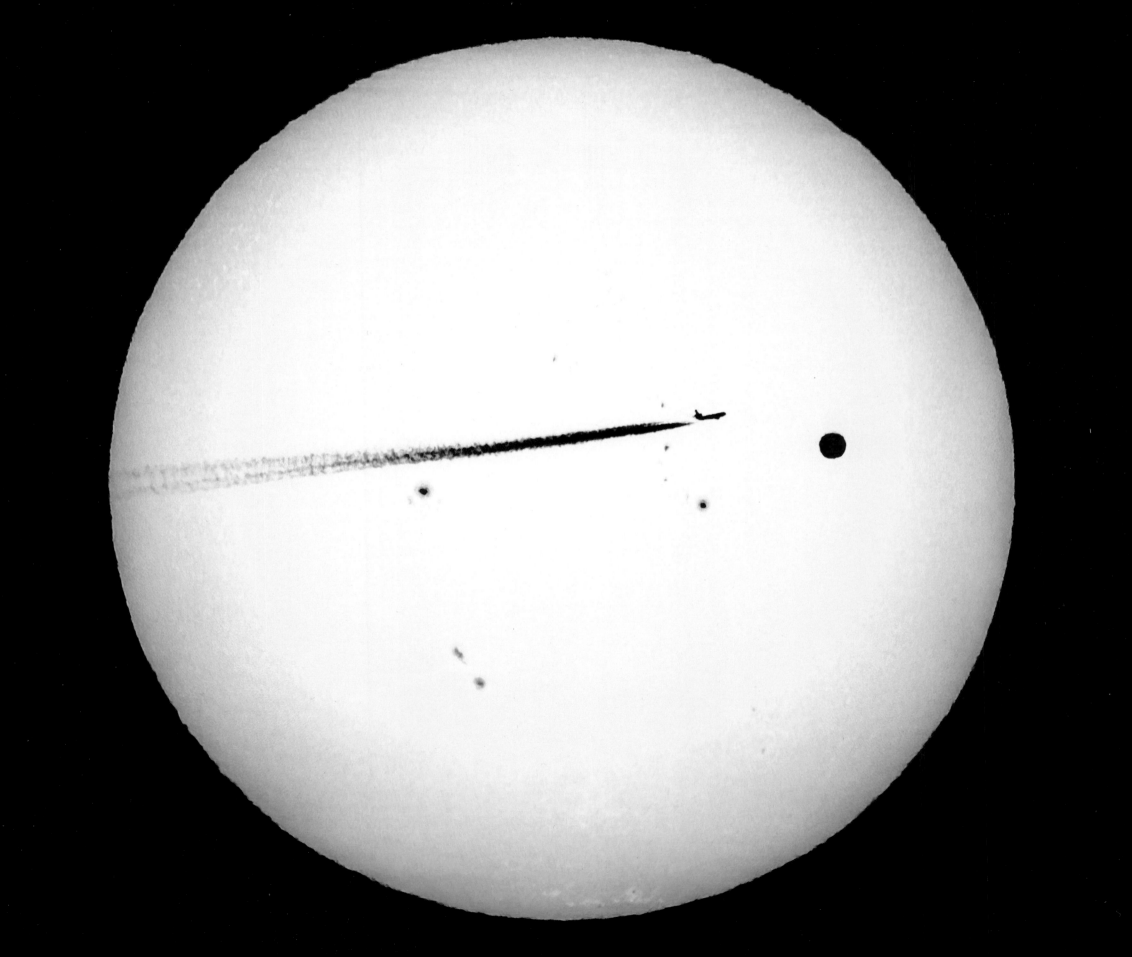

Prologue
I Was Never Much of a Runner

During tryouts for the seventh-grade track team, I was the last person to finish running the mile. They let me on the team anyway, and I ran in the hundred-meter hurdles event. In the middle of a race, the runner next to me tripped and fell over her hurdle.

I stopped midstride to ask if she was okay.

Needless to say, my running "career" was short and not very illustrious. However, the heart that prioritized that fallen runner's well-being over my finish time would stay with me forever.

In the summer of 2006, a work friend challenged me to increase my distance running. She led me through the difficult New Mexico terrain, up hills that made me feel like I'd left my lungs at the bottom, and onto longer and longer distances. I remember how wobbly my legs felt as I walked down the stairs the day after my first eight-mile run.

Over Labor Day weekend of that year, I joined my parents for a trip to Carmel, California. My family had vacationed in Carmel for many summers when I was younger, and the quaint town and beautiful Pacific coast have always felt like home to me. I shared my recent running adventures with my mom, and she said, "You know, there's a marathon in Big Sur."

We could never have foreseen what her comment would spark.

The idea took hold. "Run a marathon" had never crossed my mind. However, my twin sister had run her first one in Nagano, Japan, a few months earlier. Perhaps her feat made my attempt seem more possible. I felt good about my running, and I loved Big Sur. Besides, it was September, and the race was in April. Surely eight months was enough time to train for a marathon!

Train I did. April 2007 arrived.

At the Big Sur Race Expo, I picked up a brochure for a group called the "Seven Continents Club." Something about that club captured my imagination. Running marathons on all seven continents? That sounded *really* cool! Two days later, on the morning of the race, I had decided to join.

I completed my quest five years later, in November 2012.

The marathon adventure dominated my life for a few years. As an Air Force officer, I had a set amount of vacation days each year. Some people store up as much vacation as possible and rarely take leave. I hovered around a zero balance every year, often planning out every day of leave for the next two years. Every day was worth it.

I'm often asked why I did it. Why did I run a marathon on each continent? My first thought is, *Why not?*

From the moment the idea landed, I never looked back. I couldn't think of a single reason why *not* to do it. What an adventure it would be! It would be hard, yes, but I was no stranger to aiming high and setting my sights on the stars. After all, I had wanted to be an astronaut since the fifth grade.

Part of me thought running a marathon in a faraway land gave me an "excuse" to travel. As if "just because" wasn't a good enough reason to justify leaving work and gallivanting around the world. I thought that if I were running a marathon, I'd be making quality use of my vacation time.

I laugh about that now, my thinking I would be a slacker if I just took a regular vacation. I can see the central theme of my life from that time: the constant drive to excel, the pressure I put on myself to be perfect. I remember the desire to pause and slow down once in a while—to just be—but I also remember fearing that I would be seen as somehow "less" if I did take that time for myself. I was used to doing and doing well. I exuded the drive, motivation, and energy it takes to be an astronaut.

I wouldn't trade a moment of that part of my life for the world. It led me to where I am today; I now balance the being and the doing in a fulfilling and nourishing way. In my mind's eye, I embrace the young woman I used to be, the one who didn't know she was already enough. I thank her for her dreams. I promise her that she *is* enough and that she has the power to create her future. "Boldly go into that future," I tell her.

Looking back now at the ease and immediacy of making my decision to run the seven continents, I can see a true soul calling. I really had no doubt that I wanted to do it. I had no doubt that I *could* do it, though the how and the when and the details were a mystery. My answer was an "absolute yes" from the moment I learned about the Seven Continents Club.

In that moment, I could never have imagined—nor did I really understand during the marathon process itself—how this journey would shape the rest of my life. It was truly the journey of a lifetime. It influenced the evolution of my running style, the evolution of my lifestyle, and the evolution of my dreams.

People often ask me which race was my favorite. It's an impossible question to answer. Each stands out in its own way, carving unique trails of wonder and awe throughout my experience. Together, those trails weave a tapestry of adventure, connection, and humanity that expands and grows more beautiful every day.

Acknowledgments

If I were to name everyone whose footprints have joined mine on this journey, this book would be twice as long. Please know that even if your name isn't written, you've made a difference to me, and I'm grateful.

Thank you to the entire team at Brown Books Publishing Group who helped turn an idea into reality. Milli Brown, thank you for pioneering a new publishing model and for seeing the potential in this book. Samantha Williams, thank you for shepherding me through the process from start to finish. Thank you to Hallie Raymond for a smooth editing process and for connecting me with stellar editors. Geoffrey Norman, thank you for your enthusiasm, wit, experience, and for key suggestions that made this book stronger thematically. Katherine McClellan, thank you for your keen eye, masterful attention to detail, and for making this book stronger technically. Danny Whitworth, thank you for a beautiful cover and for thoughtful, impactful interior design. Thank you to the proofreaders, printers, binders, and everyone else involved in the process of turning life experiences into works of art.

I want to thank everyone at the Starfire Optical Range for cheering me on in my first Air Force assignment and my first steps toward marathoning. Special thanks to Christy Osmon, who took me on my first eight-mile run and turned me into just enough of a runner to believe the first marathon was possible. Thank you to Victor Esch and Troy Rhoadarmer for taking me under your wings and teaching me so much about life and leadership, both on and off the trail. Thank you to Terry Duncan, my big brother Jim Brown, Robert Johnson, Bryan Oas, Dave Wilkes, Joe Preston, John Wynia, Rob Eager, Jim Spinhirne, Kirk Meadows, Andrea Tuffli, Brian Agena, Roger Petty, Gloria Petty, Eric Weaver, Earl Spillar, Pete Cuneo, Mike Johnston, and Steven Novotny for believing in me and supporting me always. You and your families are treasured friends forever.

I want to thank Larry Wright, photographer extraordinaire, who spent hours poring over my photos and helping me select the best ones. Thank you for reminding me that the human eye-brain system has more versatility and dynamic range than any camera and for helping me share the essence of my experiences through these photos. Your insight and humor were an integral part of this book's evolution.

Thank you to Bob Fugate for driving me up the hill that day and giving me the million-dollar tour; for convincing Tom Buter to assign me to the SOR; for setting me on the path that would shape my destiny. Thank you for your enthusiasm for this project and for your inspiring photography. Thank you for that prophetic email ten years ago telling me I had a photographic eye and that these photos would become even more special in the future. I'm honored to know you.

Oleg Yakimenko, thank you for your unwavering belief in me, for helping me discover work I love, and for cheering me on every step of the way.

Eugene Bourakov, thank you for the opportunity to test your GPS in faraway lands.

Lauren Abell, Paul Oppenheimer, and Jean Ford, thank you for supporting me in key moments and beyond.

Angie Burtz, Dan Burtz, Matt Keane, Danielle Fahrenholz, Ben Overmann, and all the Protection crew, thank you for being an amazing team of humans and friends.

Susan Mashiko, Betty Sapp, the Northallerton crew, all the senior staff, Jeff Crider, Todd Benson, Scott Jacobs, Marc Herrera, Granny Smith, Barbara Barrett, Don Daly, and Helen Doerfler, thank you for opening doors of opportunity and windows of insight for which I am eternally grateful.

Sonja and Stefan Kreis, thank you for showing me what was possible.

Irina Gerasimova, thank you for asking beautiful questions at the perfect time.

Angela Clark, thank you for pancakes, stories, tears, laughter, and for being my mom's angel.

Ingrid Czintos and Samantha Treyve, thank you for deep discussions, insightful questions, mutual inspiration, and for celebrating the creative process of this book.

To my beloved Hockaday teachers, friends, and family—no amount of space would be enough to express my full gratitude and what you mean to me. To everyone I have been privileged to lead, follow, and walk beside—my piano teacher and lifelong friend, Dottie Kingston; Steve Balog and our St. Mark's AP Physics class; my Stanford professors, friends, and family; my ROTC Detachment 45 Warriors and Cadre; my Air Force friends and family; my Joint friends and family—thank you. You inspire me.

I want to thank the incredible organizers and staff of all the marathons and travel companies who enabled my journey and created unforgettable experiences, including the Big Sur Marathon Foundation, Apostolos Greek Tours, Marathon Tours & Travel, Quark Expeditions, and Albatros Travel.

Thank you to all the adventurers and runners who trained with me, whom I met in my travels, and who cheered me across finish lines, especially Ben Mathews, James Wang, Mel Buckel, Alejandro Rosally, Dan Bursch, Jim Newman, Duane Frist, Mike Looysen, Stacey Marzheuser, Sissy Witte, Don Loren, Kate Coward, Mindy Montano, Santiago de la Vega, Katja Riedel, and race rockstars Eileen M. Fannon and Andy Kinney (who should write their own books).

I want to thank the runners whose books and practices have influenced and echoed my running and life philosophies: Jeff Galloway, Christopher McDougall, Barefoot Ken Bob Saxton, Barefoot Ted McDonald, Jason Robillard, Michael Sandler, Jessica Lee, Danny Dreyer, and Katherine Dreyer.

Thank you to all the hot yoga teachers whose insight, humor, and guidance helped shape a new way of being for me. To my fellow yoga practitioners from over the years, thank you for flying together.

I want to thank Lisa Lister, Julia Cameron, Carly Stephan, and Melissa Sandon, whose soul work, wisdom, and practices led me to the creation of this book. You've helped me find my own soul work, trust my own wisdom, develop my own practices, and have faith in the magic.

To Amanda Ngui-Yen, my friend and first reader: Thank you for the miles of trails we've hiked on the earth and the many more miles we've traveled through topics and ideas that ranged all over the universe. Thank you for your insightful comments, brilliant suggestions, and for seeing it done from the start.

Thank you to my stepdaughters, Kathleen Carter and Shannon Carter, for teaching me so much. May you love your lives and find joy and fulfillment throughout your journeys.

To Jackie Carter, thank you for your love, your wisdom, your sense of humor, and your son.

I want to thank my aunts and uncles, especially Suzy Hess, Nancy Corley, Barry Schneider, and Pete Brierley, and all of my extended family, for a lifetime of love, laughter, support, birthday and holiday gatherings, staircase photos, and stories. Thank you for generously contributing to all of those marathon fundraisers! To my cousin Leslie Malz, thank you for your sense of humor, your inspiring ability to follow a plan, and for going to Rapa Nui (again) with me.

Thank you to Catherine Keefe for your beautiful soul and eternal sisterhood.

Thank you to Emily and Ian Thomsen for a wild and memorable assortment of adventures over the years. You are truly special friends, and you have always been there for me.

Thank you to my incredible Power Posse: Anne-Marie Corley, Sruti Sreerama, Gina Park, Kristen Jankowski, and Stephanie Chien. You are amazing, world-changing women and I am honored to call you my friends and sisters.

I want to thank my grandparents, whose love and precious memories will be with me forever. You shaped so much of my life. Thank you especially to my grandmother, Ann Corley, for the privilege of reading over the phone for four years.

Thank you to my parents, Dolorie and Paul Corley, who raised me with love and gave me the best possible start in life. I'm forever grateful. Thank you to my dad for inspiring in me a love of photography, a passion for science fiction, and an awe of the cosmos. Thank you for lending me your manual film camera for that high school photography class. Thank you to my mom for inspiring in me a zest for life, an eye for beauty, a creative spirit, and the seven continents journey itself. Thank you for your strength and courage. I know you would have displayed this book proudly on your coffee table. All my love, always.

I want to thank my twin sister, Anne-Marie Corley, my lifelong companion. Thank you for rescuing my China photos. Thank you for being with me at the finish line in Australia. Thank you for the big moments and the everyday, for love and laughter, for more crazy and fun conversations than I can count, for speaking in quotes, for helping each other through tough times, and for celebrating the wins. You're all I knew you'd become, and I'm so proud of you.

I want to thank my husband, Al Carter, for more than I could ever say. Thank you for believing in me, for loving me, for trusting me, for being patient with me when I was single minded and when my attention darted around like a squirrel. Thank you for keeping me fully supplied with chocolate and cake pops. Thank you for the freedom to work and for the gift of your presence and support. You make me feel incredibly loved, and you are the best partner, friend, and husband in the universe. Thank you for seeing my true heart and soul from the beginning. I love you.

And finally, to you, reader. I feel deeply blessed to be alive in this world and connected to you, whether I know you personally or not. Thank you for opening this book and bringing us together.

With love and gratitude,
Melissa Corley Carter
The Barefoot Dancing Rocket Scientist

NORTH AMERICA

Big Sur International Marathon
Big Sur, California

April 29, 2007 | April 27, 2008

The day after I finished the Big Sur International Marathon, a stranger on the street in Monterey's Cannery Row learned it was my first marathon. He told me I had guts. "You started with the hardest one!" he exclaimed.

In my mind, I started with the one that made the most sense. I started with a race in a familiar and beloved part of the United States: the gorgeous Pacific coast of California. All the Big Sur T-shirts say, "Running on the ragged edge of the Western world." It's a spectacular place.

To prepare for that first race, I used world-renowned Olympic runner Jeff Galloway's run-walk method, regularly alternating between running and walking. Most often, I'd run for five minutes and then walk for a minute. Rinse and repeat. At the time I lived in Albuquerque, New Mexico, and my training benefited from about five thousand feet of altitude and plenty of hills.

I was also blessed with an excellent support network. By the time I built up to eighteen miles—the length of my daily commute—I could run from my apartment to work. For my weekly long run, I'd drive to work, ask a friend to bring me home that evening, and then I'd run to work the next morning. My friends got a kick out of honking at me as they passed me in their cars. My training was a team effort.

My cross-training was eclectic. As a horsewoman and member of both the Albuquerque Swing and Country Dance Club and the Albuquerque Women's Soccer League, I interspersed my runs with horseback riding, dancing, and soccer. I often look back and marvel at my younger self's capacity to run twenty miles in the morning, dance for two or three hours that night, and play soccer the next day, all while taking care of my Appaloosa mare, Stormy.

I once took Stormy on a training run. My theory was that if I got tired, I could hop in the saddle and ride back to the barn. In practice, running with a horse was not the most helpful of training techniques! I spent most of the time frenetically changing my pace, trying to keep up with Stormy's quick trot or match her slower walk, all while weaving back and forth across the road as she'd lean into me or pull away. It was a fun idea, but we didn't do that again.

Unbeknownst to me at the time, Stormy laid a foundation for the evolution of my running style and my journey into mindful living. We ditched her horseshoes, and she went "barefoot." Together we practiced natural horsemanship exercises. Filling water buckets at the barn under a bright blue sky taught me the power of a pause. Stormy was the highlight of my every day and gave me an opportunity to slow down and relax from the nonstop pace of the rest of my life. Living in closer alignment with nature and experiencing and savoring the moment would later become central to my way of being.

Now . . . back to the beginning.

I didn't quite reach my full 26.2-mile distance goal while training; nevertheless, I was excited to head to California for the Big Sur International Marathon. My parents came to Carmel for a week to support me before, during, and after the race. Two of my high school friends who lived in the San Francisco Bay area came to cheer me on—they even ran the 5K!

Jeff Galloway himself ran Big Sur that year, and I was fortunate to join him and a group of other runners on Carmel Beach a couple days before the race to meet, jog, receive running form feedback, and have lunch. I also experienced what I imagine is a typical marathon nightmare. I dreamt I forgot my shoes and that I was late for the bus . . . what a disaster! How relieved I was to wake up and realize I still had one more day before the race!

The big day finally came. I remembered my shoes. I made it to the bus.

As we rode down to the start in the wee hours of the morning, I kept thinking, *Yikes, this is taking a while—and we have to run all the way back!* It was very cold as the other racers and I gathered in the starting area. Despite not yet having started my first marathon, I had already decided to join the Seven Continents Club, a prospect that warmed my enthusiasm, if not my body.

Eventually, the prerace hubbub died down, the national anthem played, a flock of white doves took to the skies, and runners cheered. I was too far back to hear the starting gun, but I knew the race was starting when everyone surged toward the start line. I finally crossed and was on my way!

The first few miles of the course took us through a beautiful redwood forest. Along the way, I noticed a barefoot runner. *Whoa!* I thought. *Running the whole marathon in bare feet?* He generated several comments from the other nearby runners. *That's pretty cool!* I thought to myself. *And he probably didn't have nightmares about forgetting his shoes.*

While the weather started out clear, it was cloudy and foggy when we emerged from the trees. It then grew windy and cold. I was glad I had trained in weather like that before, but I was a little disappointed Big Sur wasn't at its sunny best.

At first, I didn't feel the miles passing. I was beyond Mile Seven before I realized how far I'd come, and how far I had left to go. Unlike my familiar training routes, I wasn't acutely aware of what mile I was on every step of the way. Even though the weather wasn't ideal, I could hear birds, the ocean, the wind—sounds that flooded the senses and helped the time pass.

Before I knew it, I was approaching the highest point of the marathon—Hurricane Point, a whopping 590 feet—with a two-mile uphill leading to it. I could hear some taiko drummers at the hill's base infusing runners with energy for the challenging climb. I could also see a long string of runners on their way up.

I passed the drummers and clapped for them, then started up the hill. I decided to make this hill a point of pride in the marathon: I would not walk on the way up. I jogged the entire two miles uphill without following my run-walk schedule. One false summit near the top did fake me out, and I walked a few steps, but I quickly recovered and jogged the rest of the way.

On top of the aptly named Hurricane Point, I was buffeted by intense wind. When I saw a cute sign that read, "Look back at where you've been," I looked behind me and saw . . . fog. On a clear day, I could have seen the Point Sur Lighthouse I had passed a while ago. I could have seen the miles of coastline I'd just run, definitely earning the title of "the ragged edge of the Western world." The view was all fogged in today. Yet I could still see it all in my mind's eye, and I smiled and jogged on.

Happy to survive Hurricane Point, I felt great despite being very cold. As I descended the hill and neared the famous Bixby Creek Bridge, the sound of "Somewhere Over the Rainbow" reached me. The Big Sur International Marathon is renowned for its grand piano and tuxedo-clad pianist encouraging runners at this bridge, the halfway point of the marathon. As I clapped and passed by, the pianist transitioned to "Chariots of Fire" and I smiled at the classic running tune.

Though many amusing and entertaining signs kept me smiling through the miles, I started dragging. The hills after Mile Twenty grew harder and harder. My walk breaks were more frequent. Near the end, spectators advertised "free hugs," and I took advantage of the love. The Point Lobos State Reserve park rangers gave out high fives.

With about half a mile to go, I started running faster and ended up sprinting. I saw my high school friends in the crowd, and then I saw my parents cheering for me. I heard the announcer: "And #846 is Melissa Corley from Albuquerque, New Mexico. Congratulations, Melissa!" It felt fantastic to finish my journey in the welcoming arms of my family and friends.

On the whole, the marathon felt significantly more demanding than all my training runs. Still, I had crossed the finish line! I savored the sense of achievement, and I looked forward to training harder and running more marathons in the future.

I already knew which one I would run next.

I had received my second Air Force assignment. A few months later I would be posted to the Naval Postgraduate School in Monterey, California—right next door to Carmel. Why not run the Big Sur International Marathon again the following year?

I had the good fortune to train on the marathon course itself, along the Pacific Coast Highway, since I now lived in the Monterey Bay area. I shared the road with traffic on my training runs, unlike race day, when the highway is closed to cars. While the winding road and narrow shoulders didn't make this the safest option, it was an adventure that built my confidence to run on the course. Two friends of mine decided to run the marathon also, and we'd leapfrog our cars in strategic parking spots to support our one-way training on the highway.

We trained in plenty of other places: through local hills and up and down the coastal trails in Monterey, Carmel, and Pacific Grove. On one memorable day, my friend and I realized we hadn't brought enough energy-maintaining snacks on our long run. As we rounded the Asilomar coastline and entered Pacific Grove, we spotted a small shop that sold food and groceries. Neither of us had any money (a mistake we corrected on later runs). We explained our plight to the shop owner: "We've been running for eighteen miles and we're really hungry. We don't have any money, but we'll come back and pay tomorrow, we promise! May we please have a couple of snacks and some water?" The shop owner graciously took pity on us. We ate and drank, finished our twenty-three miles, and returned the next day to pay.

I'll always remember the impact of the kindness of strangers.

That wasn't the only time my fellow runners and I had unusual sustenance. I'll admit that—more than once—we strategically planned runs so we would pass by Fisherman's Wharf in Monterey to incorporate a few clam chowder samples into our moments of hunger.

By the time the race arrived, I had run on stretches of the marathon course several times and completed it end to end three weeks earlier. I was ready.

Unlike the year before, race day was gorgeous. Sunny, clear skies even prompted the next day's newspaper headline to proclaim, "Runners shine as bright as sun!" After a strong performance up the long two-mile hill, once I was on top of Hurricane Point, I looked back at where I'd been. This time I saw the beautiful coastline laid out before me.

My training paid off. I improved my time from the previous year by a full hour. I set my personal best marathon record, and it would remain my fastest.

The Big Sur International Marathon was my favorite race for high-quality training and my personal best. And, of course, it was my favorite because it was my first marathon in a beautiful place ingrained forever in my heart.

I paused to photograph the shades of blue and green during a training run on the marathon course.

Completing my first-ever marathon! Finish time: 5:45:29.
Photo by James Wang.

A road through the redwoods. Running through these majestic trees was inspiring.

Point Sur in the distance, with the Point Sur Lighthouse visible on the right. Ice plant—the succulent plant seen here in green with red tips—is a common sight in the Big Sur area. The ice plant blooms and produces a vibrant blanket of magenta flowers sometime in March.

This is the highest point of the marathon course, and aptly named! You don't want to stand too close to the edge in this wind.

Looking ahead from Hurricane Point.

Looking back from Hurricane Point. The first year I just saw fog. The second year I had a gorgeous view!

Looking down from the cliff's edge at Hurricane Point

Crossing Bixby Creek Bridge—the halfway point of the race—during my second running. Marathon finish time: 4:43:27. Photo by MarathonFoto.

The impressive Bixby Creek Bridge.

The coastline and the road—two intertwined friends who saw me through many a mile. Running on the ragged edge of the Western world indeed.

McWay Falls in Julia Pfeiffer Burns State Park. South of Big Sur, the park boasts this iconic waterfall pouring directly into the ocean.

Katy's Place, my family's favorite breakfast spot in Carmel. Delicious food and friendly service, with a line out the door most mornings and staff who remember you year after year.

♡ THANK YOU!!

Morning flowers in Yankee Point along the Big Sur coast.

Succulent plants with a lotus flower shape.

Sea nettles at the Monterey Bay Aquarium. These bright orange creatures always mesmerize me as they float serenely against a blue background.

White spotted jellyfish at the Monterey Bay Aquarium.

Yet another jellyfish variety at the aquarium. The sea produces beautifully strange creatures!

A flock of pelicans flying in formation.

Lovers Point in Pacific Grove, a popular park destination. I completed my first and only triathlon here in 2008.

Waves crashing off the coast of Asilomar.

Cypress Point on the 17-Mile Drive through Pebble Beach.

The iconic Lone Cypress on the 17-Mile Drive, silhouetted at sunset.

Cypress trees at sunset.

Waves crashing at Carmel River Beach as seagulls fly above them.

The sea green of the cresting wave contrasts beautifully with the blue at its edge.

A hawk surveys the scene.

What's that in the sand? The snowy plovers blend in so well you can almost walk right by without noticing them.

A sea otter eats some lunch in the waves at Carmel Beach. Sea otters use rocks as tools to crack open abalone shells and other tasty treats.

Clean plate club! The sea otter slurps up the rest of the meal as a wave approaches.

A great egret preens on its perch.

A male Townsend's warbler brightens up the neighborhood.

A graceful pelican in flight.

Eucalyptus trees at Mission Ranch, a farm and restaurant owned by Clint Eastwood—who was also a former mayor of Carmel.

Carmel River Beach in the morning light.

I never get tired of the vibrant colors in the water!

What my mom always called a "Hansel and Gretel" house—a lovely cottage with a wavy roof. Delightful and unique homes are plentiful in Carmel.

Dramatic morning sky at Carmel Beach.

Footprints in the sand. The journey continues!

Athens Classic Marathon
Athens, Greece
November 8, 2009

The week after completing my second Big Sur International Marathon, I put down my deposit for the first available Antarctica Marathon—two years in the future, in February 2010. Before Antarctica, though, I planned to run in Athens, Greece, in November 2009: my first race on another continent!

By the beginning of 2009, I was well into planning my intercontinental adventures. Since I would be in good marathon shape from Antarctica's race, I wanted to run China and Africa in the spring and summer of 2010. However, with a trip to see the launch of the Space Shuttle *Atlantis* in May 2009 and the Athens Classic Marathon in November, the vacation days I needed for the next two years exceeded my projected military leave balance. What was I to do?

Fate came to my rescue.

The logistics for the Antarctica Marathon changed, and there was a reduction in the number of participants allowed each year. I got bumped from 2010 to 2011. While I felt an initial panic over plans gone awry, I soon realized this allowed me the leave days I needed for both the China and Africa marathons in 2010.

In the meantime, good friends of mine introduced me to the concept of natural running and the book *Born to Run* by Christopher McDougall. I was already enthusiastic about using natural horsemanship methods with Stormy, and I had dabbled in natural swimming methods—working with the water instead of against it—while training for my one and only triathlon the year before. Natural running was, well, a "natural" progression for my training.

In the late summer of 2009, I started experimenting with barefoot and minimalist running. I knew I wouldn't run the Athens Classic Marathon barefoot, but I wanted to integrate the minimalist style into my running form as much as possible.

I experienced the standard beginner's challenges: blistering heels from ill-fitting shoes, blistering toes from poor form on a track surface, foot pain from doing too much too soon, and sore calves and Achilles tendons. Still, the idea of minimalist running called to me. I started to feel the blissful "skim" of running while connected to the earth, though that skim only lasted a few moments at a time.

Despite the challenges, my evolving running style helped me breathe easier on hills, keep better form, and feel awesome and light after runs. I was even performing better on the 1.5-mile portion of my annual Air Force fitness test. In the month before I went to Athens, I recorded my fastest 1.5-mile time yet (I would set my all-time record the following year, at 10:44). I was also crushing my hill training. When I ran a hill four times, I aimed to run successively faster each time. My goal was working.

The day of my departure for Athens arrived.

I loved Greece from the moment I saw it from the airplane, with its deep blue waters, islands, and beautiful coastline. After landing and settling in, I loved the sound of the Aegean Sea rolling in and out. Here I was, standing in a place I had only learned about from afar in my history, art, and literature classes.

Many books cover the origins of the modern marathon, so I'll summarize. In Greek, "marathon" means "where the fennel grows." Fennel was a plant revered by both the Greeks and the Romans. In 490 BC, the Greeks and Persians fought a battle on the plain of Marathon, near Athens. In an unexpected turn of events, the Greeks overpowered the Persians. Famed for the victory of a small army over a much larger force, the Battle of Marathon also gave us the tale of Phidippides. Phidippides, a Greek messenger, carried the report of victory ("Nike") across the twenty-five miles from Marathon to Athens, proclaimed Greece's win, and then died on the spot.

Fellow marathoners, take heart. Phidippides had already run to Sparta and back that week, about 150 miles each way—he wasn't killed by a single marathon. His feat did inspire the marathon event in the modern Olympics, first held in 1896. The tribute race started on the plain of Marathon and finished in the Panathinaiko Stadium in Athens. After a few Olympic Games with races of different lengths, the London Olympics of 1908 set the current race distance of 26.2 miles (42.2 kilometers).

The Olympics returned to Athens in 2004, and the marathon event once again began in Marathon and finished at the Panathinaiko Stadium. Our race course in 2009 followed that Olympic route.

To make the most of my time in Athens, I joined a tour group hosted by Apostolos Greek Tours and guest starring none other than Jeff Galloway, the run-walk guru from my previous marathon training. Early in our trip, we visited Marathon and the tomb of the Athenian soldiers who fell in battle. Having heard so much about "the plain of Marathon," I expected a big open field. Instead, olive trees dotted the landscape. As a native Texan, I was used to seeing pecans, acorns, and sweetgum balls littering the ground under their parent trees. Here in Marathon, a blanket of olives covered the ground!

I was impressed by the size of the burial mound at the tomb. One hundred and ninety-two cremated Athenian warriors and their accoutrements lay buried under the hill, yet it was even bigger than I imagined. Reflecting on the history of the place, I found myself thinking in awe about the great battle fought right where I stood. What a privilege to start our race here, to see the burial mound above the remains of ancient Greek soldiers, and to trace the messenger's steps back to the Olympic stadium in Athens.

When Jeff wasn't leading us through group training runs along the coast of the Aegean Sea, we toured the historic sites. The Acropolis stood out, of course. Home to the Parthenon—the famous structure built to protect the statue of Athena, the goddess of wisdom—the Acropolis is known as the "high city" or "the city on a hill." It is one of the most iconic symbols of Athens. On one side of the hill, at the Theatre of Dionysus, I ran my hands over the rock and marveled at how long it had been there.

We visited the ancient Agora, the historic citizens' gathering place that formed the spiritual, artistic, political, and social heart of the ancient city. We stood at the site of the House of Simon, Socrates's cobbler. "Socrates walked here" is not something you hear every day. As an American accustomed to "old" buildings being just a few hundred years old or younger, walking among structures that have stood for 2,500 years or longer was a different experience altogether.

While in the Agora, we visited the Temple of Hephaistos, the god of metalworking. I recalled him from my early years of learning Greek myths; as an enthusiastic *Star Trek* fan, I'd always loved that his Roman name was Vulcan. I'd also learned how to forge in college, thereby expanding my affinity for the smith god. The forge and the flame had always fascinated me and symbolized the fire of creativity and creation. In this historic place, I reconnected to my own ancient history.

The more we explored, the more I noticed an interesting trend: there were a lot of dogs in Athens. Our guides told us the city takes care of them and ensures they are spayed and neutered. They wear collars, but they don't belong to anyone. In the heat of the day, they particularly seemed to enjoy the shade and cool stone of the monuments and museums.

While the weather had been mostly hot and humid during our stay, race day was cold and rainy. I started the marathon wearing a trash bag as a poncho. I had experimented with adding chia seeds to my water as a source of natural energy. Chia seeds absorb water and turn into a gooey glob, and my unusual-looking water bottle drew several questions and comments like, "What the heck is *that*?!"

I wasn't alone in drawing stares. A lot of people like to dress up for marathons. In this race, one person ran the whole way dressed as a Roman centurion—complete with shield, spear, light armor, a helmet, and running shoes. A group of Texans ran in Texas flag shorts. I spotted someone wearing a red tutu and a couple wearing "Just Married" T-shirts. The back of my favorite T-shirt I ever saw read, "Dear God, please let there be someone behind me to read this!"

The race was tough, but wow . . . what a run. It was exhilarating to run in the footsteps of the ancient Greeks. Everywhere along the route, enthusiastic Greeks of all ages and all walks of life cheered us on. I had learned to say "kaliméra" ("good morning") and "efcharistó" ("thank you"), and I traded these greetings with the crowd as I ran. Even a man sheltering from the rain at a roadside vegetable stand clapped and cheered as we ran by. Cheers of "Bravo!" and "You can do it!" encouraged and energized me through the challenging run. I entertained myself by reading Greek signs and watching the road go by. From my many years studying science and engineering, and due to the pervasive use of the Greek alphabet in these subjects, I recognized many of the Greek letters on the signs.

Within sight of the Olympic Stadium, I sidetracked myself taking pictures of the changing of the ceremonial guard outside the Presidential Mansion. After that, I picked up the pace. Entering the stadium was a rush—I sprinted to the finish and passed about three people in the homestretch.

I had finished my third marathon, my first outside the United States. What a feeling! As I savored the victory and perused my souvenir poster and other mementos, I had the idea to make a collage in honor of the marathon. This collage-making became a ritual that I followed to the end of my marathon quest and beyond.

The Athens Classic Marathon was my favorite race for running in the footsteps of history. I was in awe of being in an ancient land, and I delighted in the natural and historic beauty all around me.

The Greek coastline from the air.

A sign pointing us towards the tomb of the Athenian soldiers on the plain of Marathon.

Fallen olives covered the ground in Marathon, much like acorns or pecans do in the southern United States!

An olive grove stands guard over the burial mound that covers the remains and accoutrements of 192 Athenians from the Battle of Marathon in 490 BC.

The Plaka, a dining and shopping district in Athens.

The Acropolis reflected in the windows of the Acropolis Museum. Acropolis means "city on a hill" or "the high city."

The remains of the Odeon of Herodes Atticus on the slope of the Acropolis.

The walls of the Odeon on the left with the Parthenon on the right.

The Odeon from the inside, viewed from the Acropolis.

A local dog snoozing on the steps.

The steps of the ancient amphitheater with modern Athens in the background.

The famous Parthenon, a temple for the patron goddess of Athens, Athena.

Intricate stonework on the Parthenon.

Our guide told us, "The steps look straight because they're not." Curvature was built intentionally into the steps so that, from far away, they would look straight instead of bowed in the middle. Brilliant architects!

The Erechtheion, a temple for Athena and Poseidon. The supporting columns of the "Porch of the Maidens," or "Porch of the Caryatids," are carved female figures.

Theatre of Dionysus when viewed from the Acropolis.

Hadrian's Arch in the lower left, with the Temple of Olympian Zeus in the middle. A section of the Olympic Stadium is just visible at the top left of the tree-covered hill.

Another view of the Odeon, with modern Athens above the trees.

A blue sky shining through ancient columns. I continuously caught myself staring around in wonder of this place.

The Propylaea, the official entry and exit of the Acropolis.

The ancient Agora, the historic citizens' gathering place that served as the spiritual, artistic, and social heart of Athens. Modern Athens once again makes a fascinating juxtaposition with the ancient buildings.

A Greek flag waves in the breeze.

The Marathon Flame at the race start on a grey and rainy morning.

A sign pointing the way to Athens. I loved seeing all the Greek letters on the road signs; these letters were old friends from my science and engineering classes.

Nearing the end of the race, I passed the Presidential Mansion. With the changing of the guard underway, I paused to watch the ceremony.

Homestretch in the Olympic Stadium! Marathon finish time: 5:13:38. Photo by Marathon Photos.

Savoring the finish in the Panathinaiko, or Olympic Stadium. What a view of the Olympic rings!

Greek flags flying in the stadium.

The Acropolis when viewed from the Agora, where we stretched our legs the day after the race.

Close-up of the temple and the wear of time. Little shoots of green poking through show that life always finds a way!

The Temple of Hephaistos, god of the forge and of metalworking. It was one of my favorite sites, as I am a lifelong fan of Hephaistos.

Remains of several structures in the Agora.

Simon was Socrates's cobbler. "Socrates walked here" is not something you hear every day.

The Acropolis when viewed from a local track. The Temple of Olympian Zeus is on the left of the light pole.

We found some fascinating architecture on our way through town.

The Temple of Olympian Zeus up close.

Detailed stonework on the remains of Hadrian's Arch.

Hadrian's Arch at sunset. Farewell, historic city!

ASIA

Great Wall Marathon
Tianjin, China
May 15, 2010

A week after the Athens Classic Marathon, I ran Big Sur's Half Marathon on Monterey Bay and recorded my best half marathon time: two hours and twelve minutes. I continued to practice barefoot running on my shorter distances and really started to feel like I was getting it. By Christmas, I could run three miles barefoot, and I'd figured out how to keep my barefoot form while running in shoes.

I signed up for the Big Sur International Marathon again in April 2010 to incorporate a full-distance training run about three weeks before I went to China. Unfortunately, persistent foot pain plagued my running a couple months before the marathon. I chose to take care of myself and not run the race.

I jumped into the Great Wall Marathon trip in May 2010 after not running for six weeks. I was nervous but optimistic. Unfortunately, another issue surfaced. I chose not to bring the charger for my GPS watch because I wanted to pack as lightly as possible. I would need to use the device only once, so if I brought it fully charged, I reasoned that it would stay fully charged until I needed to use it. Alas, once I arrived in China, I discovered that the watch had died. How would I time my run-walk cycles? I decided to worry about that later and just enjoy the trip.

I joined Marathon Tours & Travel, the founder of the Seven Continents Club, for my trip to China. Our group's explorations started in Beijing. We visited Tiananmen Square and the Forbidden City. There, we wandered through beautiful palaces, marveled at intricate roof and tile designs, and learned about the artifacts from different dynasties. Later in our trip we visited a zoo, a tea shop, a Buddhist temple, the old city of Hutong, and the 2008 Olympic Games sites. We ate world-famous Peking duck. We experienced a mixture of traditional culture and modern life.

Three days before the marathon, we visited the Great Wall. We would traverse the Huangyaguan, or Yellow Cliff Pass, part of the wall multiple times during the race. Due to the extreme difficulty of this section, every runner was required to hike it before the marathon.

Before we started our hike, I noticed a sign in the courtyard advertising the "Solar Eclipse Marathon" coming up in Australia in 2012. A friend and I had discussed this very eclipse a few months before! We knew it was coming, and, intrigued by the idea of seeing a total solar eclipse, we'd said we had to find an excuse to go and see it. Well, here was the perfect excuse! I wrote, "SOLAR ECLIPSE MARATHON" in my journal that night and made a mental note to sign up for it as soon as I returned home.

The hike on the wall was difficult. It was harder than I thought it would be, but it was a fun challenge (though I wouldn't exactly be calling the same stretch "fun" three days later during the marathon itself). I took it easy on the hike, often creeping sideways down the treacherously steep and

The beautiful Temple of Heaven in Beijing.

An ornate ceiling at the Temple of Heaven.

Such intricate detail and brilliant colors!

A garden on the temple grounds.

People gather in many parks across the city for tai chi and other forms of exercise. We even saw groups playing hacky sack and learning to ballroom dance!

Many forms of transportation.

The famous Tiananmen Square, packed with visitors.

A closer view of the beautiful art and architecture.

Inside the Forbidden City off of Tiananmen Square. The former Imperial Palace was closed to commoners and the public when in use as a royal residence.

Another ornate and colorful ceiling covering a long walkway.

Dragon imagery recurred throughout the city.

Each passage led to another huge courtyard within a courtyard, surrounded by elaborate buildings with beautiful rooftops, statues, and artistry.

Resilient flowers grow through the colorful roof tiles.

A small scene from a massive jade sculpture called *Da Yu Curbing the Flood*. The jade mountain carvings depict the legend of Da Yu, a king who diverted flood waters and built water-control works.

Fishing boats getting an early start in the morning.

Arriving at the Great Wall for our route preview. Are these our backup transportation methods if we get tired?

Due to the extreme difficulty of the wall section of the course—which we would run twice in the marathon—we were required to hike it beforehand. This became both a blessing and an intimidation factor. The hike healed my troubled foot—and forewarned how hard the marathon would be!

An impressive statue along our hike.

A particularly steep section of the wall! This is where I would see people crawling or climbing up using both their arms and legs during the race.

It keeps going and going . . .

A pause to appreciate the beauty of nature.

View of the valley from atop the wall.

Approaching a guard tower along the wall.

A particularly treacherous passage on the wall, with beautiful masonry. It was fascinating to see the different construction methods and materials in different sections of the wall. A bit of nature beckons in the distance.

An optical illusion! With a slight shift in perspective, an impenetrable wall becomes a navigable passage. Trust that the steps are there.

An impressive maze over the wall as we head in for the homestretch.

Yes, we are really doing this!

Recovering the next day at the zoo. Our visit wouldn't be complete without seeing a panda!

A unique assortment of pandas.

The Beijing National Stadium, or "Bird's Nest," built for the 2008 Olympic Games.

Posing with some local kids who cheered us on during the race. Photo by Sissy Witte.

Running—and still smiling—with Sissy Witte, Ironwoman extraordinaire and my lifesaver in this grueling challenge! Photo by Marathon Photos.

Crossing the finish line hand in hand with Don Loren—we made it! Marathon finish time: 7:53:22. Photo by Marathon Photos.

The old city of Hutong. Rickshaws, homes, and street-side markets filled the city.

The rickshaws had license plates! The street lights had crossing symbols for both bicycles/rickshaws and pedestrians.

The Lama Temple, a beautiful and popular Buddhist temple. Many people burn incense in the courtyard in homage to Buddha.

One of the lovely creations during a tea ceremony at a local tea shop. The flower blooms when hot water is added.

From hot water to cold water: an ice sculpture of the Great Wall adorned the buffet table at our farewell banquet. What a trip!

The "Peepee Boy." When the water is hot enough, you get the result in this image. Also, the dragon and phoenix on the cup he's standing on change color when the hot water is added.

AFRICA

Safaricom Marathon
Lewa Wildlife Conservancy, Kenya
June 26, 2010

The Safaricom Marathon in Kenya was another phenomenal experience. As it fell just six weeks after Great Wall, I didn't have a lot of time to build back my endurance from the pre-China break. However, I knew I could do anything after finishing the Great Wall Marathon.

The Safaricom Marathon was named after the mobile network operator that cosponsored the race with the conservation organization Tusk Trust. Yet the name's meaning doesn't end there. The word "safari" means "journey" in Swahili, Kenya's official language.

What a journey this was.

Once again, I joined Marathon Tours & Travel. After a brief stay in Nairobi, my fellow travelers and I headed through the countryside to spend our first few days in Africa in Aberdare National Park.

I'll never forget our first morning run through the wildlife sanctuary. We jogged with our Kenyan guides past zebras, antelopes, giraffes, and warthogs. Though the hills were challenging, I felt great. What an experience it was to run with the wildlife! Coming from a hectic life back in America, I was quickly falling under the spell of the relaxed atmosphere of this trip and the uniqueness of the land and people around me.

On the recommendation of friends, I took a tiny photo printer that connected to my digital camera. After taking photos of people, I would print out their pictures and share them. The printer was a hit! From our

running guides to our safari guides, to mothers and babies, to children at a local orphanage, I gave people their photos, and their faces lit up.

The people were an extraordinary part of this trip. We visited an orphanage in our first few days. The children there left a deep impression on us—on none more so than my roommate, Mindy Montano. The story of the Safaricom Marathon isn't complete without the story of what Mindy did next. In the inset, hear from Mindy about the nonprofit organization she created to help the children we met: Kids of Kenya and Kieni West.

We'd been at Aberdare Country Club for a day or two, and I had decided to lie down for an hour or so to rest. While I was napping, Melissa came in and said she and some others in the group were going to walk down the road with an Aberdare employee to visit a children's home. I jumped up and put my shoes on, saying, "Hang on, I'm coming with you."

We walked about half a mile down the road to a rundown, neglected orphanage that a woman and her late husband had started in their own home. Despite the conditions in which the children lived, they greeted us with song and dance. As I observed both the children dancing and those watching, I made eye contact with a young boy. From that moment, I knew there was no turning back. He was the sign that it was my calling to do something for those children. I created Kids of Kenya and Kieni West upon my return to the United States that summer.

My goal was to help the children achieve a life with better access to more opportunities. How better to do that than with education? Sending the children to school became the main goal of Kids of Kenya and Kieni West. Now, ten years later, we have two college graduates. Eunice graduated in 2018 with a nursing degree and is now a nurse in a small town in Kenya. David graduated from Nyeri National Polytechnic in 2019 with an accounting degree. We have two students currently enrolled in college: John is working toward a degree in procurement, and Margaret is halfway through her journey at pharmaceutical school. We have three students about to enroll in college: Christine and Veronica will begin their degrees in hotel hospitality, and Jeremy will begin his studies in electronics.

More will follow in their footsteps.

Never did I think that a trip to Kenya to run a half marathon would lead to major changes in my life and the lives of orphans whom I now consider family.

—Mindy Montano

HelpingKidsOfKenya.org

Where it all started . . . Mindy with the kids in 2010.

Mindy with Eunice Njama at Eunice's college graduation in 2018.

Mindy with David Mwangi Wachira in 2018. David graduated college the following year.

The wildlife we encountered left a deep impression as well. We joked that this marathon was perfect for anyone who has ever said they would run only if something were chasing them. Thankfully, the only things that chased us during our training runs and the marathon were other runners. But we delighted in the safaris we took and the animals we spotted along the way, from elephants and Cape buffalo to rhinos and lions.

We had one special day at the Ark, a boat-shaped lodge within Aberdare National Park. Amazingly enough, my dad had stayed at this place thirty-five years earlier on a trip to Africa with his parents. The Ark overlooks a watering hole and salt lick that attracts a wide variety of animals. In addition to the plentiful elephants and buffalo during the day, we saw hyenas in the evening and kept our eyes peeled for the rare leopard. Though we didn't see a leopard, my enthusiasm was undimmed. The spectacular views and comical elephant antics were more than enough to feel the fullness of the experience.

We also took a side excursion to see the Ark from far away. We clung to the vehicle as we traversed rugged terrain, and our safari truck even got stuck in the mud. An eagle-eyed passenger spotted a massive elephant in the forest that we almost missed because we were so focused on the road ahead. What a metaphor for life; it's important to pause and appreciate what's right in front of us. We can stay connected to the long-term vision while also remaining present in the moment that's unfolding right now. After finding many more elephants, we turned around and made our way back to the Ark, arriving in one piece. What a ride!

Back at our first lodge, I roamed freely about the grounds, startling a warthog here and there, just taking in the beauty all around me. We experienced the magic of a night game drive and ended our visit with a traditional bush dinner. When we left the next day, our new friends waved goodbye, and I felt sad to leave. I hadn't quite realized what an effect this place and these people had had on me in the past few days.

We traveled through beautiful and rugged countryside as we headed for our marathon site, the Lewa Wildlife Conservancy. This trip took us directly across the equator. Though I'd crossed the equator in the air before, I'd never crossed it on the ground. I stood under the marker sign and smiled.

I reflected on my journey as I sat on the bus after the equator adventure. This journey had progressed at a slower pace, allowing me more freedom and downtime than I had had in China. I had packed in many wonderful and new experiences. In China, the marathon itself dominated my experience. On this trip, the marathon would be the icing on the cake.

I had run among wildlife, learned about Kenya and Africa, and expanded my awareness of the world and its vastly different resources, opportunities, and people. Not for the first time, I felt deeply how fortunate my life was and how fortunate I was to connect with those who were different from me. Celebrating our common humanity was the true essence of this trip.

We finally arrived at our home for the marathon: a safari camp in the Lewa Wildlife Conservancy. Our previous lodgings in the jungle gave way to tents and bucket showers on the savanna. After an exciting "bush run" through the preserve, I took my first bucket shower. I learned that one doesn't actually need that much water to take a shower. I had more than enough in that bucket, enough even to wash my long hair. Once again, I appreciated the opportunity to reflect on what "enough" looks and feels like and to recognize how much I took for granted. I savored the luxury of simplicity.

I felt the need to pinch myself on our safari: What an experience! Our Maasai guide, Laban, taught us about the wildlife on the savanna. He taught us how a Grévy's zebra differs from the common zebra because of its narrower stripes and bigger ears. We learned that the pattern on a reticulated giraffe is more defined than on other kinds of giraffes. We saw Grant's gazelles, velvet monkeys, oryx, and rock hyraxes, small animals about the size of a squirrel that, amazingly enough, are distantly related to the elephant. We saw a male ostrich dancing back and forth trying to impress a female. The landscape and the wildlife were spectacular.

On a late afternoon game drive, we embarked on a mad chase when Laban spotted three zebras running in the distance. At first he thought a jackal was chasing them. Next, he thought it was a jackal chasing gazelles. Then: "It's a cheetah, hang on!" He revved the engine and we screamed over to the next ridge. Squatting on the hood of the vehicle, he searched for the cheetah through his binoculars. He didn't find the cheetah, but he did find lions!

Our guide informed the safari network. Every safari vehicle in the area converged on the lions. Even though I enjoyed taking photos, I noticed how touristy we seemed. I wondered what the animals felt in that moment. They seemed fairly nonchalant. A lioness lying on a fallen tree branch looked at each vehicle in turn, sat up, yawned, stretched, and flopped back down again. Three other lions lay in the grass nearby, expertly camouflaged in the tall brown grass. A young male gazed at us, his little mane just beginning to grow.

Feeling contemplative and excited to have seen lions, we returned to camp and ate our last dinner before the marathon. That night, I was thrilled to see the Southern Cross constellation, visible only in the southern hemisphere. A full moon rose. I didn't know it then, but the nighttime areas of the world would see a lunar eclipse as we ran the next day.

On our way to the start line on race day, we saw a zebra and a giraffe run across the road. The full moon was setting and a beautiful sunrise greeted us. Life was complete.

I felt great during the first half of the two-lap course. The hills were no problem. Amusingly, the race leader lapped me when I was on Mile Ten—meaning he must have been on Mile Twenty-three! The second half of the marathon proved more difficult and took me over twice as long as the first half. Despite the increasing challenge, it felt glorious to find myself alone a few times on the savanna with no runners ahead of or behind me. I savored the feelings of freedom and connection to the earth.

As I came in for the finish, I smiled as the race support crew cheered and clapped, encouraging the runners enthusiastically. Though I was exhausted and covered in dust, I laughed when I saw monkeys grabbing boxes of orange juice at the finish line.

My experience in Africa was unique and inspiring in so many ways. I was in constant awe of my proximity to the natural world around me, witnessing that instinctive and intuitive connection of humanity to nature. A fellow marathoner summed up this symbiotic feeling with a phrase he heard from the Kenyans he ran with: "You must thank that hill. Because of that hill, you are a better runner."

The Safaricom Marathon was my favorite race for the remarkable people, landscapes, and wildlife with whom I shared the journey. Thank you, hill. Thank you for making me better.

Giraffes and zebras during our first morning run.

Running with the wildlife—an amazing experience!
Photo by a fellow traveler.

Arthur, one of our running guides.

Charlie, another running guide.

James, one of our intrepid safari guides.

We met a few mothers and babies on our way to the Kieni West Children's Home. This beautiful mother had a precious smile and a precious child.

Someone brought lollipops and handed them out—
they were a hit with the children!

I took photos of each mother and child and printed
them out using a mini portable printer.

A mother and child looking at their photo. I love the contemplative look on this child's face and his mother's smile as she watches him.

The forested landscape of Aberdare National Park.

A male Cape buffalo who's been playing in the mud.

A female Cape buffalo and her calf.

A female bushbuck watches us.

The warthogs mostly showed us their backs.

Heading deeper into the forest.

We almost missed this elephant! It's hard to believe. We were too focused on the road ahead. This encounter was my reminder to notice what's actually around me. It's great to have a vision, but you can only get there from *here* and *now*.

The watering hole at the Ark, the boat-shaped lodge where we stayed for one night. Elephants and buffalo were the most populous visitors, but we saw others as well—even some hyenas at night!

An elephant rises out of the water. You can see the mud lines that show how deep it was standing.

Splish splash, this one's been taking a bath!

An elephant family. You can spot the relatively tiny legs of a baby behind the mother.

Is this elephant about to eat a buffalo? It's all a matter of perspective.

Cape buffalo watching us watching them in front of the Ark.

Back at the main part of Aberdare National Park, giraffes lounge, impalas graze, and warthogs trot away. I loved seeing all the animals together.

While on the road from Aberdare National Park to the Lewa Wildlife Conservancy, we crossed the equator!

Beautiful cloth art at a shop we visited.

From the forest to the savanna we go. We arrived in the Lewa Wildlife Conservancy, where the marathon was held.

Dramatic trees reach toward a blue sky.

This looks like a scene from *The Lion King*.

A reticulated giraffe, with pronounced dividing lines between the patches of brown. What a gorgeous coat!

Grant's gazelles on the alert.

Grévy's zebras have larger ears and thinner stripes than the "common" zebra, with white bellies where the stripes stop. They are the most endangered species of zebra.

Another Grévy's zebra poses for the camera.

Grévy's and common zebras together. Can you tell the difference?

Our home for the next couple of days.

Common zebras grazing in the morning. A kori bustard, one of the largest flying birds, lingers nearby.

The white rhino, named not for its color but for its wide mouth. A white rhino's back also looks like a popular resting place for birds.

A wide mouth, indeed.

Beautiful reflections in this serene watering hole.

Feeling constantly in awe of the beautiful and wild landscape.

An acacia tree with a fungus that makes the trunk turn orange. It doesn't hurt the tree.

Ants live in the bulbs in a symbiotic relationship with acacia trees.

After a wild chase searching for a cheetah, we found lions instead. A thrilling find! This lioness surveys the scene.

Shifting perspective.

Getting comfortable, still watchful.

So over it. Your photographs are wearing me out!

As a full moon set, this gorgeous sunrise greeted us on race morning! Unbeknownst to me at the time, race day saw a partial lunar eclipse in the dark time zones.

And we're off! Tiny figures against the vast savanna.

Homestretch in the wildlife park! Marathon finish time: 6:24:36. Photo by Karen Bronstein.

The dust of the miles. These shoes used to be light blue! Like many other runners, I chose to leave my race shoes behind to donate to those in need. What a true "safari" this trip was. An amazing journey indeed.

ANTARCTICA

Antarctica Marathon
King George Island, Antarctica
February 28, 2011

Three months after the Safaricom Marathon, I earned my astronautical engineering PhD and moved to Chantilly, Virginia, for my next Air Force assignment. Fate had rescued me in more ways than one with the delay of the Antarctica Marathon to 2011. Preparation for this unique race was all about training with the proper weather and mindset.

The temperate Monterey climate would not have prepared me well for the challenges of Antarctica. I didn't expect Virginia's weather to be much more helpful, but it actually surprised me. The winter there—colder than most I had lived through in Texas, California, and New Mexico—taught me the ins and outs of running in wind, snow, and ice. I also learned what clothing and gear worked best for me. I prefer to be too hot during a race rather than starting out cold, so I always layer up. With gloves, a combination hood and face mask, thermal top layers covered by a wind-resistant outer shell, leggings under wind-resistant pants, and thick socks inside my thin-soled "barefoot" boots, I could coast through a winter run no matter how windy it was. I grew confident that, with the right preparation, I could *weather* any weather.

I trained in a nearby national park. A variety of trails snaked through the park, and each weekend I'd create a course that would provide the mileage I needed for my long run. As I familiarized myself with the trails and returned to them regularly, whisperings of insight from past and present running experiences crystalized into an epiphany. Again, baby steps.

Starting each long run was intimidating. After the first mile, I'd think, "Gosh, so many miles to go . . . the finish line is so far away." Yet I continued to put one foot in front of the other, over and over again. I repeated mantras from my barefoot running books, like, "Easy, light, smooth, fast, relax, relax, relax." I'd look at my watch and notice, "Wow—only one mile to go!"

All that stands between Mile One and "only one mile to go" is a series of steps. "One mile to go" always arrives. This insight always reminded me that everything was possible.

Prepared by winter weather, improved mindset, and three years of anticipation, I set out eagerly on my journey to the ends of the earth. I was about to begin the experience of a lifetime!

I joined Marathon Tours & Travel for the third time. The trip started with an abrupt return to summer: three days in Buenos Aires, Argentina. February is hot throughout most of the southern hemisphere! My roommate from the Great Wall Marathon would be my roommate on this trip as well. While in Buenos Aires, we relaxed, toured the city, ran a few miles, and met fellow travelers. On the day before we traveled to Antarctica, several of us took an impromptu ferry ride across the river to Colonia, Uruguay.

The colorful La Boca neighborhood of
Buenos Aires, Argentina.

A picturesque street in Colonia, Uruguay. We
took a ferry from Argentina, crossed the river,
and spent the day here.

Puerto Madero, a magical find in Colonia. These fruits and veggies went straight into our meals! I enjoyed resurrecting my Spanish to act as interpreter between our group and the café staff—and even some other non-Spanish-speaking tourists!

Flowers after a refreshing rain.

Another beautiful flower graced with raindrops.

A delightful cobblestone street in this quaint little town, seen from a fun angle.

Arriving in Ushuaia, or the "end of the world." We set sail to Antarctica from here.

On our day at sea crossing the Drake Passage, I quoted Robert Cushman Murphy in my journal: "I now belong to a higher cult of mortals, for I have seen the albatross!"

Gentoo penguins on our first land stop in Antarctica, the Aitcho Islands.

Feeding time! The acrobatic transfer of regurgitated fish from parent to chick.

Penguins dotting the whole landscape, with surprising green in the background. I didn't expect to see green in Antarctica!

Chinstrap penguins. The extra-feathery ones are molting.

A humpback whale in Nelson Strait!

At the race start on King George Island. We would run by this location several times because it was a multilap course. We piled up our water bottles in preparation.

Even through the mud and desolation, I'm smiling behind the mask! Marathon finish time: 6 hours. Photo by Katja Riedel.

The mud I collected during the run. I wasn't sure if these pants would ever be clean again.

The next morning, after crossing the Bransfield Strait, we awoke to the idyllic image of Antarctica.

Gorgeous morning light on the icebergs.

I was in awe of the deep blue sky, the pure white snow, and pockets of crystal blue here and there.

Incredible snow-covered mountains as we approached Cuverville Island.

Iconic Antarctica: penguins and icebergs. What could be better?

A fuzzy gentoo penguin chick on Cuverville Island.

The Lone Penguin.

Different kinds of algae add these amazing colors.

Watch out, this penguin looks angry! Who will win this staring contest?

We could actually hear the ice shifting and cracking. It made an incredible sound.

A Zodiac looking very small as it cruises through Neko Harbor. We rode these inflatable rafts between the ship and the shore for all our landings.

A crabeater seal snoozes on the tip of the iceberg. You can see the rest of the ice under the water!

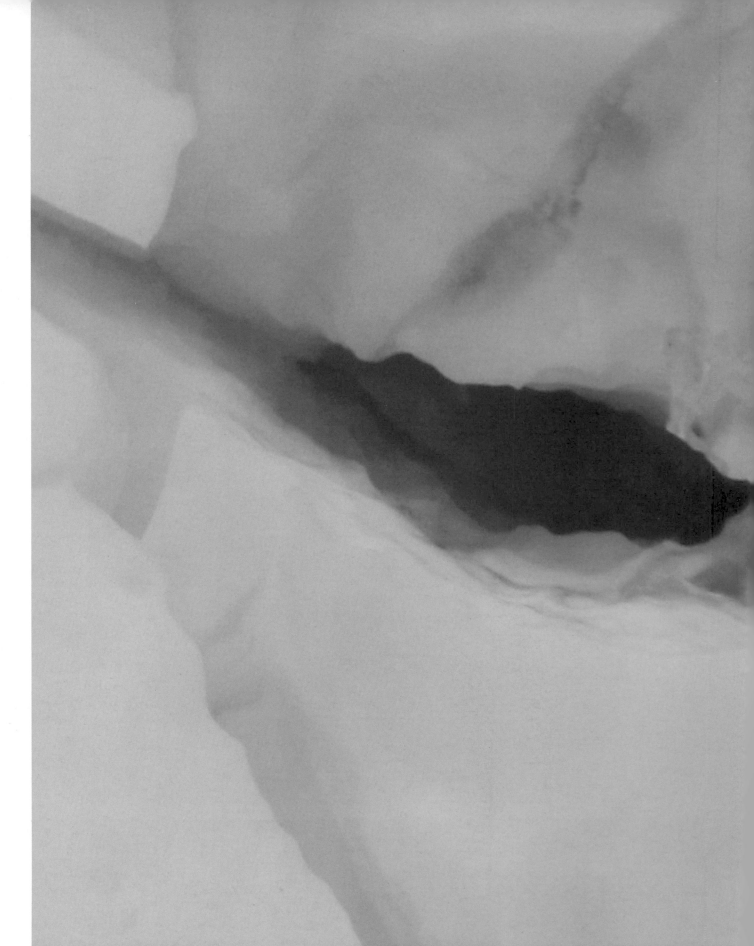

The deep crystal blues in the
ice were breathtaking.

Landing on the Antarctic continent in Neko Harbor.

Icicles melting into water droplets.

Take me with you!

Penguin highway.

Looking a little bedraggled.

An iceberg floats alone below a blanket of clouds.

An ice shelf of pristine beauty.

I've taken many an ice bath after a marathon or long run. I like to think this chick is icing its wings after a long, hard swim.

A gorgeous mountain towering over the ship and a tobogganing penguin below. Maybe it's just resting.

Water so clear you can see this penguin's feet!

Delicate, yet hardy, ice crystals.

Port Lockroy, a British base housing a small museum, a gift shop, the southernmost operational post office in the world, and the all-important issuer of passport stamps.

Cruising through the Lemaire Channel to arrive at Petermann Island, the southernmost point of our journey.

We hiked to the southern point of the island. The wind at the point felt like we were running the marathon again. At the other end of the island, we saw a few Adélie penguins, the third species of penguin we encountered on this trip!

Simply breathtaking.

The magic continued on a Zodiac cruise through Pleneau Bay, the "iceberg graveyard." Icebergs of all shapes and sizes have drifted here from near and far; some have even run aground and rolled over. You can see where this iceberg's water line used to be.

We were filled with wonder and awe to be in this spectacular place.

Stunning shades of blue. Amazing patterns in the ice.

Fascinating shapes rise above this snoozing crabeater seal.

From one Zodiac to another, through the looking glass . . . or the iceberg arch.

The winds were gusting quite a bit and the sea was rough. Everyone got wet in this honorary polar plunge!

The "South American plunge"—we dove into the frigid waters of the Beagle Channel as we returned to Ushuaia. Each swimmer was connected to the ship by a safety rope. The water was definitely cold enough to count as a polar plunge! What a fitting farewell for this amazing journey. Photo by Alexandra Burgar.

SOUTH AMERICA

Rapa Nui Marathon
Rapa Nui (Easter Island), Chile
June 3, 2012

Six weeks before the Rapa Nui (Easter Island) Marathon, my twenty-year dream to become an astronaut came to a shattering end.

Yes, I was one of those kids. I had wanted to be an astronaut ever since an astronaut came and spoke to my fifth-grade science class. I was the space geek who grew up watching *Star Trek* and *Star Wars* with wide-eyed wonder. I attended every level of Space Camp. To this day, I can tell you the names of the original Mercury Seven astronauts and the order in which they launched.

Though writing and literature analysis always came more naturally to me, I loaded up on math and science in high school. I graduated from Stanford with a bachelor's degree in mechanical engineering, a master's degree in aeronautics and astronautics, and a commission as an officer in the United States Air Force. Despite having far-from-acceptable vision by NASA standards, I kept working toward my dream. I earned my PhD in astronautical engineering and could actually say I was a rocket scientist. When NASA started accepting candidates who had received corrective eye surgery, I got LASIK. When I began running marathons, I set a new goal for myself: become the first person to run a marathon on all seven continents *and* on the International Space Station.

Finally, the day came to call on all I had accomplished. I applied to be an astronaut in January 2012. Despite thousands of people applying for very few slots, I truly believed I had a chance. I felt giddy just hitting the "apply" button. This was it! I was chasing my dream!

I received the news in April: I was rejected on medical grounds. Despite my post-LASIK 20/20 vision, my pre-LASIK eyesight was bad enough to disqualify me.

To say that I was devastated is an understatement.

I wrote pages and pages of reflections in the days that followed. I called my family and friends and I cried. A lot. I put all my *Star Trek* DVDs out of sight because I cried every time I looked at them. I didn't know what to do, and I couldn't imagine how to move forward.

I know that part of my devastation came from fear. I had wrapped up so much of my identity in this astronaut dream that I didn't know who I would be or what I would do without it. I had told everyone I'd ever met that I wanted to be an astronaut. Most of them told me that they could absolutely see me doing that job and that I would be perfect for it. What would I tell those people now? Could this really be it? Wasn't there one more person I could convince, one more thing I could try? I'd grown up believing I could do anything I set my mind to, and I truly believed I would make it into the NASA Astronaut Corps. I was riding high in the sky on all that I'd achieved. Crashing back to earth was a reality check I never thought I would have to face.

It seems fitting that I ended up in this remote, mystical, and magical place after a soul-crushing experience and the death of my own status quo. The transformation from death to life—symbolized by Easter itself—and the spiritual power and life force of the universe—represented by the island's mysteries and monuments—renewed and energized me.

Looking back now, with decades of life experience, I realize that my fifth-grade self was steeped in the visuals, language, and inspiration of space travel. I believe I channeled my soul's innate desire for cosmic connection into the more tangible idea of becoming an astronaut. Though my eyesight closed the astronaut door, my eyes were opened to a greater *vision* that led me straight home to myself.

I now live in that energy my soul has called me toward all my life. I embrace what I call "the goal behind the goal"—what I *really* wanted when I set my sights on the stars all those years ago. I wanted to be a part of something bigger than myself and inspire others to shine their own light, just like astronauts had always inspired me.

The Rapa Nui Marathon was my favorite race for transformation, embracing mystery, and going barefoot. It opened my heart to the mystery of the next stage of my life. It called me home to the earth. It called me home to the universe inside of and all around me.

It rained a lot on our first day in Chile. I slipped and fell flat on the pavement in my enthusiasm to take this photo.

A view of Santiago, Chile, from San Cristóbal Hill. You can see the snow-covered Andes Mountains in the distance and a reflective tower in the city.

The "Devil's Cellar" at Concha y Toro, a winery we visited.

Old architecture on Santa Lucía Hill in Santiago.

My cousin Leslie and I pose on Santa Lucía Hill with Santiago and the Andes in the background. Photo by a fellow traveler.

Colorful homes built on the steep hills of the port city of Valparaíso, Chile.

La Casa de Pablo Neruda, a Chilean poet. The inside was just as unique as the outside. A blue sky shines bright, creating a bold background for the colorful house.

As in Athens, dogs in Chile were plentiful. We would find the same situation later on Rapa Nui—where each dog had its own territory.

Arrival in Rapa Nui! Welcome to island life.

A horse grazes among the palm trees.

The remains of a boat-shaped house.

All the *moai* on the island were toppled by the late 1800s; many were toppled onto their faces. Those that stand have been restored. This one has been toppled on its back. As a wave crashes, the *moai* looks like it is exhaling.

Ahu Tongariki, where fifteen *moai* are restored—the most *moai* standing together on the island. The platform beneath the *moai* is called the *ahu*. The stone artwork is a massive feat of engineering all around! Those horses look so small in comparison to the statues.

The red *pukao*, or topknots, were carved separately and placed on top of the *moai*. Various theories exist about what the topknots mean and how they were elevated into place. The red volcanic rock came from Puna Pau, a different quarry from where the *moai* were carved.

Such an incredible sight.

The *moai* dwarf the humans, and the sky dwarfs the *moai*. I was perpetually in awe of this strange and magical place as I stood in the presence of these monuments.

Ahu Tongariki when viewed from another *moai*. A tiny person in front of the *ahu* lends some perspective.

This *moai* most likely never stood up at all—no eye sockets were carved out, and the eyes were carved after the *moai* was placed on the *ahu*. The eyes were made of coral and are a rare find. It is believed that some *moai* fell during the transportation to their destinations and were left where they fell.

Rano Raraku, the quarry where the *moai* were carved. Rano Raraku is one of the three extinct volcanoes forming the triangle shape of Rapa Nui.

Moai on the slope of Rano Raraku. The heads have bodies that have been buried by years and years of erosion.

This *moai* is still connected to the mother rock. It looks like it is taking a nap.

A very old *moai* at Rano Raraku, with Ahu Tongariki in the distance.

I joined the *moai* in watching the rainbow.

Moai at Anakena beach, the marathon's turnaround point. They have a dramatic silhouette!

Te Pito o Te Henua—"the navel of the world," or, as I like to translate it, the "womb of the universe." The whole island is sometimes referred to as Te Pito o Te Henua, but this is the belly button itself. Many people come here for various spiritual experiences, and the magic of the site holds deep meaning for me. The nearby *moai* is probably the most ignored one on the island.

It was fascinating to see the differences in the *moais'* facial features. The *moai* are believed to have represented specific people, with features representative of their subjects.

Anakena beach itself. A beautiful beach and a warm swim.

The ever-present wind blowing through the palm trees.

Wild horses roamed the island freely.

Such a peaceful and serene setting. It is mind boggling to contemplate everything that was created and all that has taken place on this island over the centuries.

Restored dwellings at Orongo, the ceremonial village associated with the *Tangata Manu*, or Birdman cult, which arose after the time of the *moai*. Which door to choose?

The crater of Rano Kau, another of the volcanoes forming the triangular shape of Rapa Nui and yet another place where I was overwhelmed by the natural beauty.

A view from Orongo Village. In the *Tangata Manu* ceremony, competitors swam to the farthest island with the goal of retrieving the first egg of the season laid by the *manutara*, or sooty tern. The chief of the winner's tribe became the overall leader and a sacred person for a year, and the winner's tribe had the highest standing.

Cave paintings from the *Tangata Manu* period depicting the *manutara*.

A petroglyph from the *Tangata Manu* period, with the slope of Rano Kau in the background.

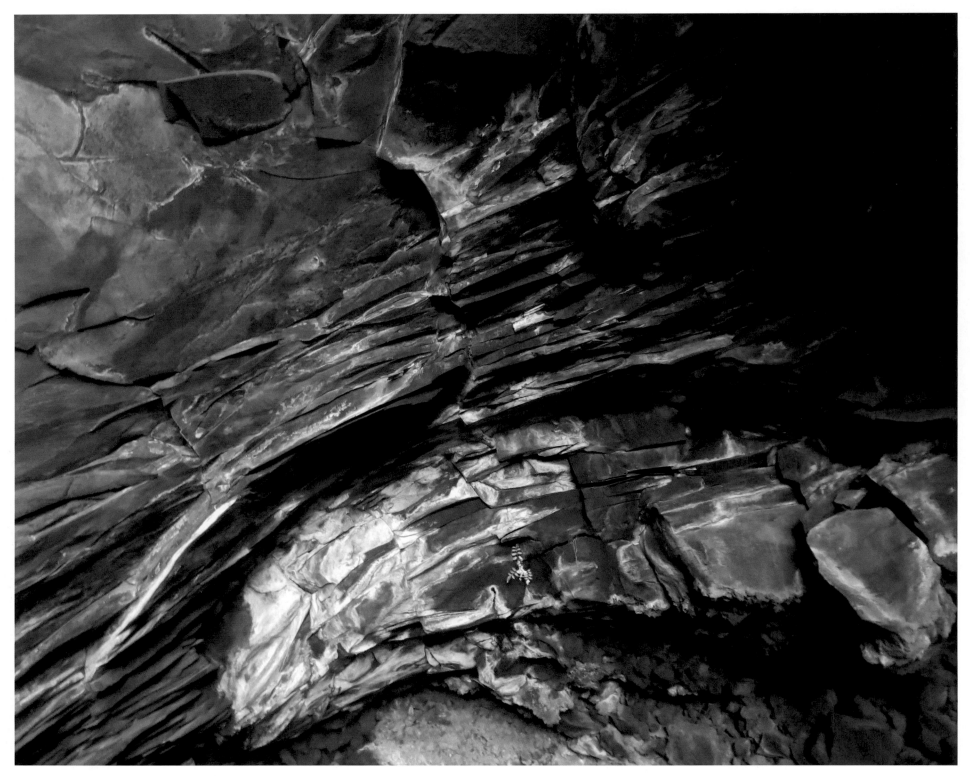

Art in nature—fascinating rock formations inside the cave.

The colorful cemetery of Hanga Roa, with a mixture of native and Christian symbolism. Hanga Roa is the island's only town.

Moai in the background of the cemetery. You can see that the coral eyes of the one on the right have been recreated and placed in the eye sockets. This was a timely theme for me, as eyesight gave way to the greater importance of vision in my life.

Dogs snoozing in the shadow of the *moai*.

My barefoot finish on the island of mystery! I ran about three miles barefoot over the course of the race. Marathon finish time: 6:10:07. Photo by Cheryl Tabaracci Higgins.

We went on a horseback ride for our postrace recovery. An adorable wild foal watched us curiously.

This is a cairn built at the highest point of Ma´unga Terevaka, the third volcano in the Rapa Nui triangle. This volcano also happened to be the summit of our horseback ride. A distant rainstorm over the ocean lends an intense feel to the already wild landscape.

A herd of wild horses cruises across the road on our return. What did they think of their domesticated counterparts, and vice versa?

Our final sunrise on Rapa Nui. Farewell, beautiful island, and thank you!

OCEANIA

Solar Eclipse Marathon
Port Douglas, Australia
November 14, 2012

Falling just a few months after the Rapa Nui Marathon, the Solar Eclipse Marathon in Australia was both the perfect follow-up and a fitting conclusion to my epic seven continents journey. The race was timed with a total solar eclipse. We would start as soon as the sun's rays emerged from behind the moon. This marathon would be unique in its cosmic significance.

This event also presented a mammoth hill challenge. Unlike the other races I had run, with their rolling hills or steady inclines and declines, the Solar Eclipse course was mostly flat. It featured one notable exception: the "bump track." The course's elevation profile looked something like a top hat. The bump track rose from about sea level to an elevation of 1,200 feet over the span of about a mile. This massive hill was twice the elevation of Big Sur's Hurricane Point—with half the climb distance.

While I didn't have this elevation profile in my local area, I continued to train in the national park. The trails had served me well for my races on the last two continents and would continue to do so. I ran hill repeats on a short but steep hill, challenging myself to run faster each time. I rallied my physical and mental energy while going up longer hills, knowing the bump track would be even harder. Finishing the marathon had always been more important to me than the finish time itself, and that was certainly true here. I trained with one goal in mind: run well on the bump track.

Three weeks before Australia's Solar Eclipse Marathon, I ran the Marine Corps Marathon for my full-distance training run. While the course itself was mostly flat, it did boast a slightly uphill homestretch. As an Air Force officer, I particularly enjoyed the patriotic flavor of this run and the iconic finish at the Iwo Jima Memorial in Arlington National Cemetery.

After a brief stop in Dallas, Texas, to visit my parents and grandparents, my sister and I boarded the plane for Australia. She would join me for this culminating event and run the half marathon herself. We would also meet up with Eileen M. Fannon, a friend I had made at the Great Wall Marathon, who brought along her own posse of running friends.

Albatros Travel was our marathon and tour organizer for this trip. We landed in Cairns, Australia, and rode a bus up the scenic coastline to Port Douglas, our race destination. On our first morning in Australia, we took a boat from Port Douglas out to the Great Barrier Reef. We marveled at the waves breaking in the distance. They broke not against an island but against the reef itself. The deep blue of the ocean here was unlike anything I had ever seen. Antarctica amazed me with its crystalline, cold blue waters. Australia's waters were a warm blue, bright and sparkly and inviting.

We arrived at the activity platform—a launching point for snorkeling, diving, and underwater observation. The different depths of water reflected

A serene morning in Port Douglas, Australia. Ready for a trip to the Great Barrier Reef!

On the activity platform. This crystal blue water was as bright as that of Antarctica, but it was warm instead of cold!

As we snorkeled through the area, we saw many kinds of coral, including staghorn, brain, and plate.

The black-and-white sergeant major fish were everywhere. Though they are not in this photo, we also saw clownfish and sea turtles on our excursion.

Boat wakes have always mesmerized me, showing where we've been and where we're headed.

A rainbow lorikeet at the Wildlife Habitat we visited. I marveled at lorikeets just like these living in the wild in Port Douglas.

Double-eyed fig parrot. An adorable little thing!

The majestic yellow-tailed black cockatoo.

A pied heron in the wetlands habitat.

A laughing kookaburra. Someone tell a joke!

A cattle egret with breeding season coloring around the beak and eyes.

The glossy ibis.

Birds walking on the canvas ceiling when viewed from inside. What a pattern they created!

Quite the attitude from the bush stone curlew.

Like a puppy, this chick has some feet to grow into!

We watched this mother purple swamphen catch a fish, tear it into pieces, and feed it to her three chicks.

A black-necked stork with her chicks.

A lovely flower interlude.

A yellow-billed spoonbill preening.
Quite a bill indeed!

The flightless cassowary. This bird
amazed me with its prehistoric flair.
It doesn't look real, but it is. Looking
at this creature, I could easily believe
that birds are dinosaurs.

That's not a rock; it's another prehistoric-looking creature, the crocodile.

A smoke ceremony welcoming us to the Mossman Gorge area of the Daintree Rainforest. "Go with good spirit."

A beautiful fern in the rain forest.

Lush and varied vegetation.

A bent tree pointing the way, as our guide described. It acts as a reminder that the path of life runs true even if it doesn't run straight.

The Mossman River that created Mossman Gorge.

Manjal Dimbi, the mountain that holds back the evil spirit. It was named by the Kuku Yalanji people in honor of Kubirri, who protected them from the evil spirit Wurrumbu.

The beautiful bird of paradise flower.

The windy beach on the evening before the marathon.

The sunrise over the ocean on race morning. Runners collect on the beach, awaiting the eclipse.

Just before the start of the eclipse.

Despite the clouds, we experienced the dramatic and sudden darkness of the eclipse's totality.

Let there be light! It amazed me how quickly the smallest sliver of sun lit up the world again. We were then off to the races!

The last step of my seven continents marathon journey and the first step of the rest of my life. Marathon finish time: 6:02:32. Photo by Marathon Photos.

Twin race medals! My sister completed the half marathon and celebrated with me at the finish line. She even had the race announcer say that I was finishing my seventh continent. Thanks, Sis! Photo by Eileen M. Fannon.

Participating in Andy Kinney's finish line tradition, because 26.2 miles wasn't enough of a workout. Andy also finished his seven continents journey with this race! Photo by Anne-Marie Corley.

Our last morning in Port Douglas—a gorgeous day.

A unique—and daunting—sign at the beach. We stayed respectfully far away from the water. This sign was enough to deter me from taking a dip.

The curved trees give the feel of a hug.

Farewell, beautiful Port Douglas! Thank you for the amazing experience!

© 2017 by Robert Q. Fugate. Taken August 21, 2017, from Unity, Oregon. Though our Australian eclipse was mostly cloudy, this is what a total solar eclipse can look like. The sun's outer layer, the corona, brilliantly flashes into view as the moon covers the disc of the sun. A few solar prominences are visible around the edge. A beautiful sight! Photo printed with permission.

A tribute to an epic journey. My seven continents race medals were framed by Cindy
Gummer at the Enchanted Galleries, Dallas, Texas.

Epilogue

Reader, perhaps you've wondered, "What's up with the hills?" I asked that same question as I revisited my journals and training logs and saw the hill theme emerge again and again.

It took me asking myself that question and then jogging up a few local hills to discover the root of their magic.

Hills are manageable chunks. They're discrete, distinct, doable, visible. They inspire clarity of purpose. They reward focused effort with rest. Hills welcome the celebration of wins big and small. They honor and embrace the mystery of the future without creating paralysis in the present. They invite the breaking up of a giant leap into a series of small steps.

Completing the seven continents was the crest of a hill for me, and I rested and celebrated at the top.

When my astronaut dream shattered, I felt like I was in a valley with hills rising in every direction. In a marathon, I knew which hill to climb. In life, I had no idea.

I drifted for a few years without a big career goal. Those on the outside might not have believed I was just drifting; I still had a great career in the Air Force, and I was going places. Even though I settled into life on a path that still looked like traditional "success," my heart started to wander. I took small steps in a few different directions. I read emerging and ancient wisdom on topics like mindfulness, living with intention, redefining success, and thriving. I envisioned a life of meaning and fulfillment, where I could skyrocket love, compassion, and kindness in the world.

Sometimes the giant leap is choosing which small step comes next, choosing which hill is next. If we're really courageous, the leap is trusting the universe to show us. It's trusting that we have all the resources we need to create our most vibrant future.

Five years later, in 2017, I had transitioned from active duty to the Air Force Reserve, where I taught leadership and professional development courses through the lens of mindfulness. I had become a certified life and leadership coach and started my own business. I had married an amazing man and begun a new journey with him. I had integrated all the phases of my life, and I felt purposeful and peaceful.

But that year, a moment of deep grief still surfaced. Watching *Apollo 13* during a leadership class launched me into a sobbing fit and yet another existential crisis of faith and identity. I thought I had recovered. What could still be wrong?

My own stellar life coach helped me realize that it wasn't the pain of not being an astronaut that I was still holding on to. I had learned from my pain. What I needed to release was fear. I was actually afraid of *being okay* with not being an astronaut. I was afraid of being fully healed.

This was a new twist in my identity crisis. Five years earlier, I didn't know who I would be if I wasn't the sure-bet aspiring astronaut. Now a part of me—albeit a small part—didn't know who I would be if I wasn't the *recovering* aspiring astronaut.

What if I could tell a new story altogether? What if I could simply be whole? What if I could simply *be*? My next step leaped out at me.

I had helped others—and even myself—reframe deep issues, disappointments, challenges, and regrets through the healing power of gratitude. Yet it hadn't occurred to me until that conversation with my coach to write a "gratitude letter" to my astronaut dream.

Regularly expressing gratitude for joyful moments is a life-changing step in and of itself. Finding gratitude in challenging circumstances, situations, and relationships changes the game even more. It shifts us into a whole new world. It helps us create a new reality.

To my astronaut dream, I wrote:

"Excellence is the result of caring more than others think is wise, risking more than others think is safe, dreaming more than others think is practical, and expecting more than others think is possible."

Thank you for inspiring me to excel through a lifetime of following and living by these ideals.

Thank you for accompanying me for so many years, and for the incredible experiences that I will treasure always . . . from Space Camp to the Air Force, from Apollo 13 to Interstellar, for the values of integrity, service, and excellence, for world travels and inner journeys . . . you are an eternal source of joy and inspiration.

Thank you for the belief that you were possible. Thank you for the sheer exhilaration and giddiness of hitting that "apply" button.

Thank you for helping me aim for the stars and inspiring me to achieve remarkable things. Thank you for giving me the confidence, courage, and skills to arrive at a crossroads, recognize the difference between doing and being, and to choose "the road less traveled by."

Thank you for freeing me to pursue my underlying dreams and to reach my stars in other ways.

I see you, and I see that you are not me. You are an integral part of me, and you shaped a huge portion of my life, but I am greater than you. I am more than you. When you were shattered, a friend said, "When people tell you how they can picture you being an astronaut, it's because they see something so great and wonderful within you that no dream seems beyond you."

Success isn't being an astronaut. It's being that person for whom no dream is impossible.

Thank you for my success.

Since writing that letter, I've continued to learn, grow, and let go. I've continued to find deep meaning in my experiences, knowing that every experience illuminates our unique place in the cosmic tapestry. I've come to know myself as the Barefoot Dancing Rocket Scientist, a champion of resilience.

Resilience actually *is* rocket science. In fact, everything is rocket science in the end. Running. Life. In essence, they're all about going from where you are to where you want to be, acknowledging progress and adjusting course, and letting go to lift off.

Therein lies the unification. The marathon journey and the astronaut journey were synergistic threads in the tapestry my soul weaves in collaboration with the universe. Those journeys were key elements of a larger pattern and purpose: to build grounded leaders, connected humans, and powerful teams that change the world. I hope my story will shine a light for others, inspiring them to heal and shine their own light. I hope that, together, we'll forge a brighter future for all of humanity.

One step at a time. One hill at a time. That's how we change a life, change the world, and create the future.

Today, running and life swirl together, images flashing by. I remember blazing confidently up the most challenging hill and then stopping to wonder, "Am I on the right track?" I remember backtracking a little and learning to trust.

In running and in life, we accept help, and we reach out to help someone else. We come to realize that we can complete a challenge better together. When we pause, we notice that what we've been chasing is already here. We see the world from a new perspective. Learn from pain. Release our fear.

We have faith in that tiny sliver of light and know that it is enough to transform the darkness.

I see us all, facing seemingly impossible dreams, goals, projects, and situations by simply putting one foot in front of the other over and over again, creating a series of small steps that weave back and forth and up and down, leading us straight to our dreams.

I remember that the run *is* the win.

About the Author

Photo by Mina Habibi.

A rocket scientist and Air Force officer turned writer, artist, leadership coach, and resilience champion, Melissa Corley Carter builds grounded leaders, connected humans, and powerful teams that change the world. A certified professional coach who holds two engineering degrees from Stanford University, an MBA from the University of New Mexico, and an astronautical engineering PhD from the Naval Postgraduate School, Melissa brings a unique blend of soft skills and technical expertise to her work. A firm believer that resilience actually *is* rocket science, Melissa helps people go from where they are to where they want to be. She encourages others to acknowledge their progress, adjust course, and let go to lift off.

A minimalist running enthusiast and hot yoga practitioner, Melissa also loves creating collages, hand-crafting unique greeting cards, and photographing wildlife, landscapes, seasons, and other forms of progression. She dances with the universe daily and joyfully embodies her soul's journey as the Barefoot Dancing Rocket Scientist.